NETFLIX

STRANGER THINGS

THE OFFICIAL COLORING BOOK

WELCOME
TO
HAWKINS

NETFLIX

STRANGER THINGS

THE OFFICIAL COLORING BOOK

TEN SPEED PRESS
California | New York

Coca-Cola

All Friends Welcome
Castle Byers
All Friends Welcome
Home of Will the Wise
Castle Byers
Home of Will the Wise

PENTAX
PENTAX
PENTAX
PENTAX
PENTAX
PENTAX

HAWKINS
POWER AND LIGHT

Starcourt
Starcourt

YOU RULE
YOU SUCK
YOU RULE
YOU SUCK
YOU RULE
YOU SUCK
YOU RULE
YOU SUCK
YOU RULE
YOU SUCK
Robin

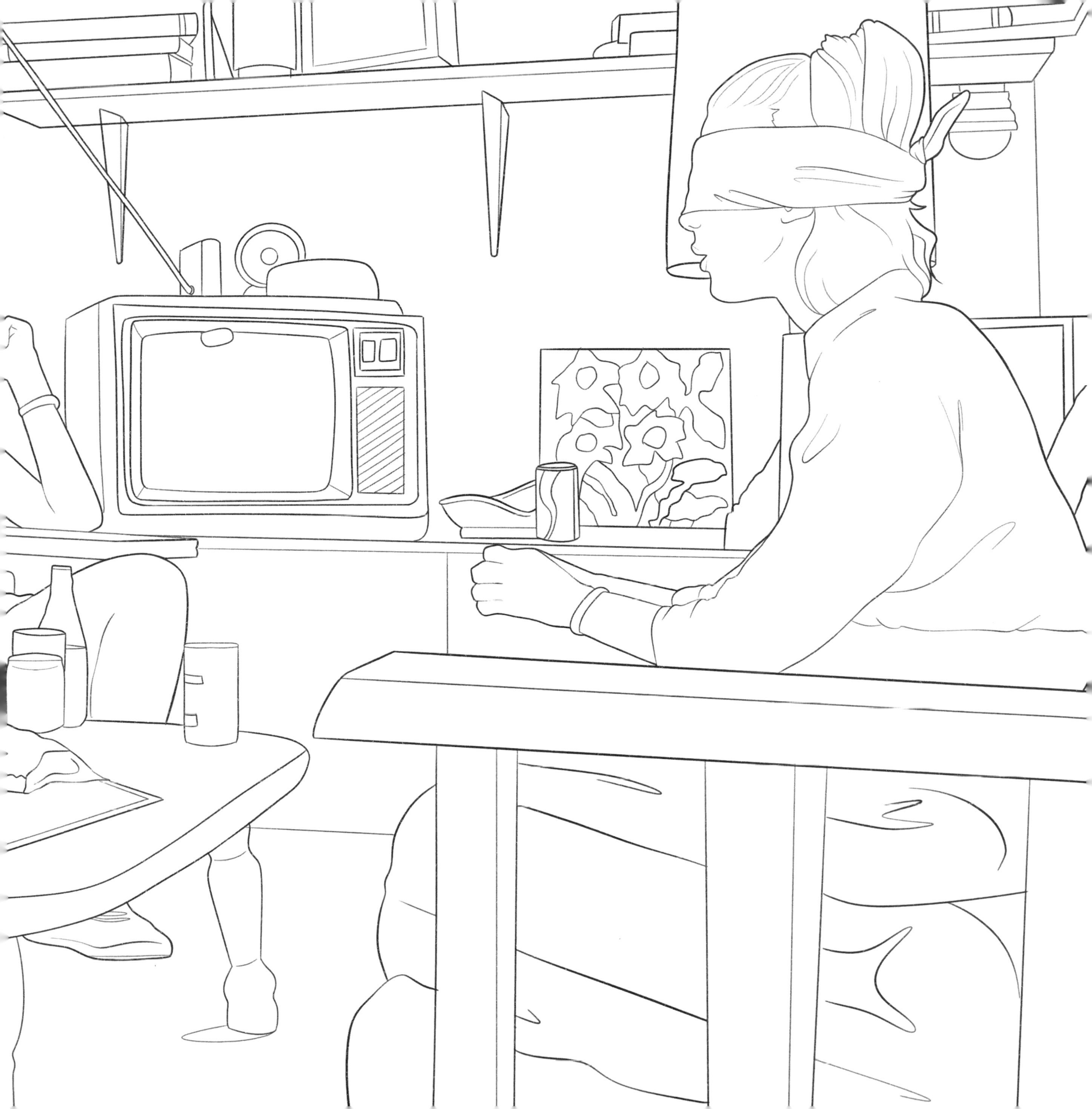

AHOY
AHOY
Robin
Steve
SCOOPS AHOY

1UP
1UP

ARCADE

FUN FAIR

Eggo
8 Homestyle
Waffles
Eggo
8 Homestyle
Waffles

3 MUSKETEERS
DEMODOG
DEMODOG
3 MUSKETEERS

A B C D E F G H
I J K L M N O P Q
R S T U V W X Y Z

Snow

Ball

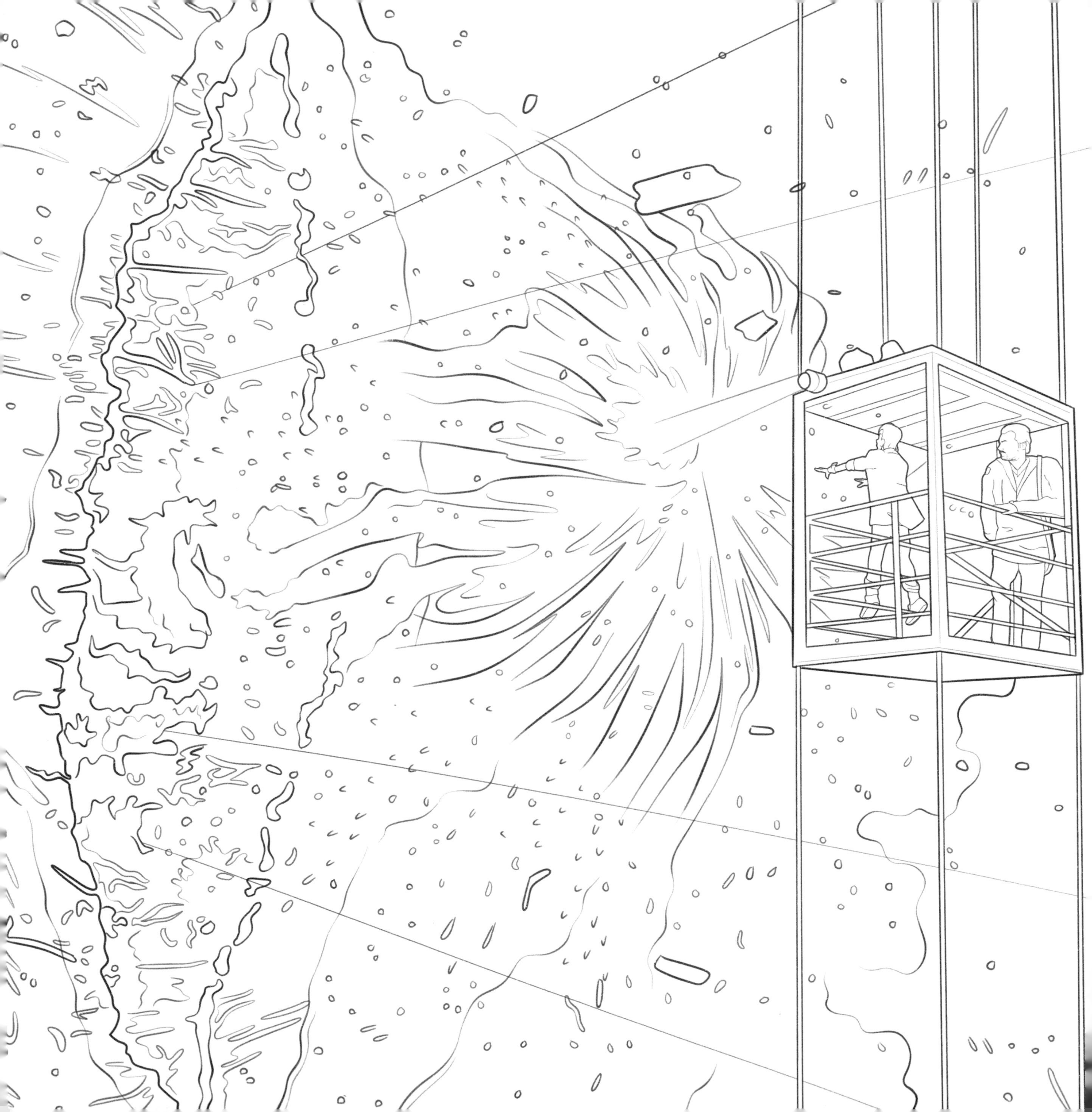

FRIENDS DON'T LIE

FRIENDS DON'T LIE

starcourt

Starcourt
Mall
HAS IT ALL!

Tigers
GO TIGERS!
HAWKINS
1
9
8
6
HIGH SCHOOL
Hawkins
Hawkins
GO TIGERS!
Tigers

HAWKINS
POLICE
STATE OF
INDIANA
CHIEF
380

Surfer Boy Pizza
Surfer Boy
Pizza
Surfer Boy Pizza
Surfer Boy
Pizza
Surfer Boy Pizza
Surfer Boy
Pizza
Surfer Boy Pizza
Surfer Boy
Pizza
Surfer Boy Pizza
Surfer Boy
Pizza
Surfer Boy Pizza
Surfer Boy
Surfer Boy Pizza
Surfer Boy
Pizza
Surfer Boy Pizza
Surfer Boy
Pizza
Boy Pizza
Surfer Boy
Pizza

HELLFIRE CLUB
HELLFIRE CLUB
HELLFIRE CLUB
HELLFIRE CLUB
HELLFIRE CLUB
HELLFIRE CLUB
HELLFIRE CLUB

CAMP
'85
KNOW WHERE

DEMOBAT
SLAYER

DEMOGORGON
HUNTER

SILENT
60
5
10
15
20
25
30
35
40
45
50
55

RINK-O-MANIA
ROLLER SKATING

THINKING
CAP

ROLL FOR YOUR
LIFE
DICE DON'T DIE

UPSIDE DOWN